# SETTING MY MORAL COMPASS

# GROUP DIRECTORY

Pass this Directory around and have your Group Members
fill in their names and phone numbers

**Name**

**Phone**

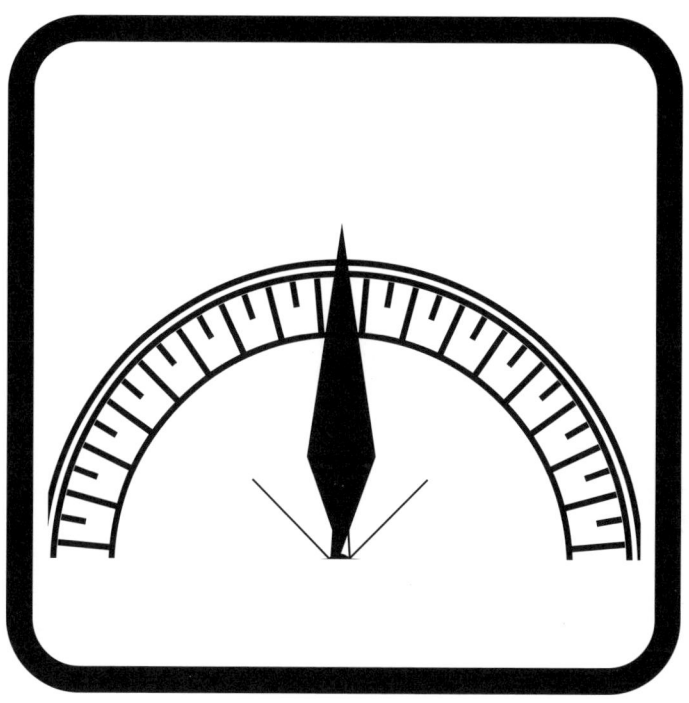

# SETTING MY MORAL COMPASS

**EDITING AND PRODUCTION TEAM:**
James F. Couch, Jr., Lyman Coleman, Sharon Penington, Cathy Tardif,
Christopher Werner, Matthew Lockhart, Erika Tiepel,
Richard Peace, Andrew Sloan, Scott Lee

NASHVILLE, TENNESSEE

© 2003, 1998, 1988 Serendipity House
All rights reserved
Printed in the United States of America


Published by Serendipity House Publishers
Nashville, Tennessee

International Standard Book Number: 1-57494-303-0


ACKNOWLEDGMENTS

Scripture quotations are taken from the Holman Christian Standard Bible,
© Copyright 2000 by Holman Bible Publishers. Used by permission.


Nashville, Tennessee
1-800-525-9563
www.serendipityhouse.com

# TABLE OF CONTENTS

| SESSION | REFERENCE | SUBJECT | PAGE |
|---|---|---|---|
| 1 | Matthew 5:1–12 | Character | 11 |
| 2 | Romans 8:5–17 | Morality | 19 |
| 3 | Matthew 5:38–48 | Unconditional Love | 25 |
| 4 | Galatians 5:16–26 | Spirituality | 31 |
| 5 | Matthew 6:19–34 | Contentment | 39 |
| 6 | James 4:1–12 | Relationships | 47 |
| 7 | Matthew 7:13–27 | Choices | 55 |

# CORE VALUES

**Community:** The purpose of this curriculum is to build community within the body of believers around Jesus Christ.

**Group Process:** To build community, the curriculum must be designed to take a group through a step-by-step process of sharing your story with one another.

**Interactive Bible Study:** To share your "story," the approach to Scripture in the curriculum needs to be open-ended and right brain—to "level the playing field" and encourage everyone to share.

**Developmental Stages:** To provide a healthy program throughout the four stages of the life cycle of a group, the curriculum needs to offer courses on three levels of commitment: (1) Beginner Level—low-level entry, high structure, to level the playing field; (2) Growth Level—deeper Bible study, flexible structure, to encourage group accountability; (3) Discipleship Level—in-depth Bible study, open structure, to move the group into high gear.

**Target Audiences:** To build community throughout the culture of the church, the curriculum needs to be flexible, adaptable and transferable into the structure of the average church.

**Mission:** To expand the Kingdom of God one person at a time by filling the "empty chair." (We add an extra chair to each group session to remind us of our mission.)

# INTRODUCTION

Each healthy small group will move through various stages as it matures.

## STAGE ONE

**Birth Stage:** This is the time in which group members form relationships and begin to develop community. The group will spend more time in icebreaker exercises, relational Bible study and covenant building.

## STAGE TWO

**Growth Stage:** Here the group begins to care for one another as it learns to apply what they learn through Bible study, worship and prayer.

## STAGE FOUR

**Multiply Stage:** The group begins the multiplication process. Members pray about their involvement in new groups. The "new" groups begin the life cycle again with the Birth Stage.

## STAGE THREE

**Develop Stage:** The inductive Bible study deepens while the group members discover and develop gifts and skills. The group explores ways to invite their neighbors and coworkers to group meetings.

**Subgrouping:** If you have nine or more people at a meeting, Serendipity recommends you divide into subgroups of 3–6 for the Bible study. Ask one person to be the leader of each subgroup and to follow the directions for the Bible study. After 30 minutes, the Group Leader will call "time" and ask all subgroups to come together for the Caring Time.

# Each group meeting should include all parts of the "three-part agenda."

**Ice-Breaker:** Fun, history-giving questions are designed to warm the group and to build understanding about the other group members. You can choose to use all of the Ice-Breaker questions, especially if there is a new group member that will need help in feeling comfortable with the group.

**Bible Study:** The heart of each meeting is the reading and examination of the Bible. The questions are open, discover questions that lead to further inquiry. Reference notes are provided to give everyone a "level playing field." The emphasis is on understanding what the Bible says and applying the truth to real life. The questions for each session build. There is always at least one "going deeper" question provided. You should always leave time for the last of the "questions for interaction." Should you choose, you can use the optional "going deeper" question to satisfy the desire for the challenging questions in groups that have been together for a while.

**Caring Time:** All study should point us to actions. Each session ends with prayer and direction in caring for the needs of the group members. You can choose between several questions. You should always pray for the "empty chair." Who do you know that could fill that void in your group?

**SHARING YOUR STORY:** These sessions are designed for members to share a little of their personal lives each time. Through a number of special techniques, each member is encouraged to move from low risk, less personal sharing to higher risk responses. This helps develop the sense of community and facilitates caregiving.

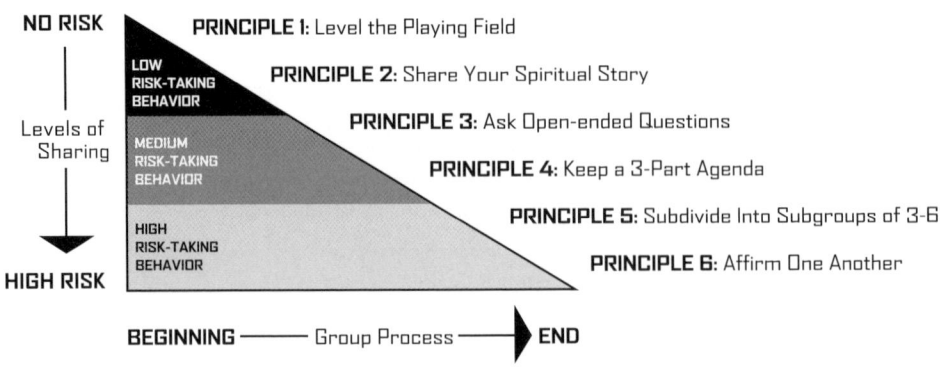

**GROUP COVENANT:** A group covenant is a "contract" that spells out your expectations and the ground rules for your group. It's very important that your group discuss these issues—preferably as part of the first session.

## GROUND RULES:

- **Priority:** While you are in the group, you give the group meeting priority.
- **Participation:** Everyone participates and no one dominates.
- **Respect:** Everyone is given the right to their own opinion and all questions are encouraged and respected.
- **Confidentiality:** Anything that is said in the meeting is never repeated outside the meeting.
- **Empty Chair:** The group stays open to new people at every meeting.
- **Support:** Permission is given to call upon each other in time of need—even in the middle of the night.
- **Advice Giving:** Unsolicited advice is not allowed.
- **Mission:** We agree to do everything in our power to start a new group as our mission.

## ISSUES:

- The time and place this group is going to meet is _____
- Refreshments are _____ responsibility.
- Child care is _____ responsibility.

# Session 1

## Scripture **Matthew 5:1–12**

 Welcome to this course on discovering our core values and developing a Christlike character. In our studies, we will look at some of the ways Scripture challenges our perspective and our thinking. We will reevaluate the way we look at the world and see if others are drawn to Jesus through what we say and do.

Scripture offers us the road map by which to set our moral compass. It can open our eyes to see things from God's point of view, rather than the world's point of view. It shows us a new and beautiful paradigm. The word "paradigm" is a Greek word, and means the way in which we perceive, understand and interpret the world around us. This new way of looking at things can help us change from the inside out.

Once we change from the inside out, then how we function and respond in the world (our character and our motives) will also change. We will live in accordance with God's will in spite of the influence of the culture surrounding us. As a result, we will achieve a true spiritual joy, instead of just happiness. Spiritual joy is eternal; happiness is temporal. This joy is based on spiritual realities; happiness is based on earthly circumstances. Spiritual joy is an inner reality; happiness is dependent on external events. Together let us seek to find the true joy and abundant life that is promised to all who follow Jesus.

Every session in this course has three parts: (1) **Ice-Breaker**—to get to know each other better and introduce the topic; (2) **Bible Study**—to share your life through a passage of Scripture, and (3) **Caring Time**—to share prayer concerns and pray for one another.

## Ice-Breaker : 15 min.
# CONNECT WITH YOUR GROUP

**Leader**
Be sure to read the introductory pages in the front of this book prior to this first session. Remember to stick to the three-part agenda and the time allowed for each segment. To help your group members get acquainted, have each person introduce him or herself and then take turns responding to the Ice-Breaker activity.

There would probably be no better way to get to know a person's character and values than to follow him or her around for a day. Since we can't do that, we'll do the next best thing—share what a typical day in our life is like. Take turns completing the following sentences.

1. Generally it's best not to talk to me in the morning before ...
   ○ I've had my cup of coffee.
   ○ I've read my paper.
   ○ I've had my shower.
   ○ noon!
   ○ No problem—I'm a morning person.
   ○ Other_____.

2. The high point of my day is when ...
   ○ my kids go to school.
   ○ my kids come home.
   ○ my spouse comes home.
   ○ I come home.
   ○ I get to delve into my pet project.
   ○ I talk to my friend(s).
   ○ I get to eat.
   ○ Other_____.

3. An important part of ending my day is ...
   ○ watching a favorite TV show.
   ○ watching the news.
   ○ prayer and quiet time.
   ○ reflecting on the day with my spouse.
   ○ watching the sunset.
   ○ reading.
   ○ Other_____.

## Bible Study : 30 min.
# READ SCRIPTURE + DISCUSS

**Leader**
Ask two group members, selected ahead of time, to read aloud the Scripture passage. Then discuss the Questions for Interaction, dividing into subgroups of three to six. Be sure to save at least 15 minutes for the Caring Time.

Jesus focuses on the character and actions that should mark those who are his disciples. He begins with what are known as the Beatitudes that describe what kind of person God wants each of us to be, and the rewards such a person can expect. Read Matthew 5:1–12 and note how these blessings differ from what the world values.

**The Beatitudes**

Reader One: 5 *When He saw the crowds, He went up on the mountain, and after He sat down, His disciples came to Him.* ²*Then He began to teach them, saying:*

Reader Two: ³*Blessed are the poor in spirit, because the kingdom of heaven is theirs.*

Reader One: ⁴*Blessed are those who mourn, because they will be comforted.*

Reader Two: ⁵*Blessed are the gentle, because they will inherit the earth.*

Reader One: ⁶*Blessed are those who hunger and thirst for righteousness, because they will be filled.*

Reader Two: ⁷*Blessed are the merciful, because they will be shown mercy.*

Reader One: ⁸*Blessed are the pure in heart, because they will see God.*

Reader Two: ⁹*Blessed are the peacemakers, because they will be called sons of God.*

Reader One: ¹⁰*Blessed are those who are persecuted for righteousness, because the kingdom of heaven is theirs.*

Reader Two: ¹¹"Blessed are you when they insult you and persecute you, and say every kind of evil against you falsely because of Me.

Reader Two: ¹²Be glad and rejoice, because your reward is great in heaven. For that is how they persecuted the prophets who were before you.

**Matthew 5:1–12**

 **QUESTIONS FOR INTERACTION**

**Leader**
Refer to the Study Notes at the conclusion of this session as needed. If 30 minutes is not enough time to answer all of the questions in this section, conclude the Bible Study by answering question 7.

1. Imagine you were sitting on the hillside that day with the disciples. What would have been your first reaction to hearing Jesus' words?
   ○ "What on earth is he talking about?"
   ○ "This guy doesn't live in the real world."
   ○ "Jesus had better change his message—because he won't get very far preaching that stuff."
   ○ "This lifestyle is what I've been searching for."
   ○ Other_____.

2. What do you think it means, as a Christian, to be "poor in spirit," "mourning" and being "persecuted"?

3. The word "blessed" is often translated as "happy" or "healthy." How does living out the Beatitudes lead to happiness and health?

4. How does the promise that you will receive a great reward in heaven (v. 12) give you courage and perseverance in this life? What happens if you lose that perspective?

14

5. Silently take an "attitude check" by placing the appropriate number (from 1 to 4) in the space next to each beatitude.
   (1) "I'm just beginning."   (3) "I've experienced this."
   (2) "I'm making progress."  (4) "This is part of my life."

   ____ POOR IN SPIRIT: I recognize my spiritual bankruptcy and my need for God.

   ____ MOURN: I feel the pain that sin, including my own, causes. I can let others know when I'm hurting without embarrassment.

   ____ GENTLE: I don't have to be the strong one who is always in control. I can be tender and meek.

   ____ SPIRITUAL HUNGER: I want to know God and his will for my life more than anything. My heart truly longs for God.

   ____ MERCIFUL: God has given me sensitivity for the suffering of others and a compassion to help them.

   ____ PURE IN HEART: I'm completely honest with God and others. My life is marked with openness and integrity.

   ____ PEACEMAKER: I work hard to keep channels of communication open with others. I help those around me work out their differences without hurting one another.

   ____ PERSECUTION: I'm willing to suffer and (if need be) stand alone for what is right. I can take criticism without reacting defensively or feeling self-pity.

6. Share with the group which beatitude you would rate as your highest and which beatitude you would rate as your lowest.

7. What do you need to change in order for your life to reflect the Beatitudes?
   ○ I need to change the way I view the world.
   ○ I need to change my attitude.
   ○ I need to change my behavior.
   ○ I need to change my circumstances.
   ○ I need to continue what I'm doing, since my life already reflects the Beatitudes.
   ○ Other_____.

## GOING DEEPER:
If your group has time and/or wants a challenge, go on to these questions.

8. Are the Beatitudes applicable to life today, or only to the lives of Jesus' audience? Do you think it's harder to follow the Beatitudes in today's world than it was in Jesus' day? Why or why not?

9. Do you think we are always called to be peacemakers? Is there ever a time when war is justified?

Caring Time : 15 min.
## APPLY THE LESSON AND PRAY FOR ONE ANOTHER

**Leader**
Go over the group covenant found at the beginning of this book. At the close, pass around your books and have everyone sign the Group Directory.

Take time to express your concern for each other as group members by praying for one another.

1. Agree on the group covenant found in the introductory pages.

2. Have the group pray for your lowest rated beatitude in question 5.

3. Share any other prayer requests and then pray, asking God to lead you to someone to fill the empty chair (see the introductory pages).

## NEXT WEEK

Today we heard Jesus define in the Beatitudes the character that is to be formed in his disciples. We were reminded that we must change from the inside out and be ready to live differently than those influenced by the world. In the coming week, evaluate how you fulfilled the Beatitudes each day and pray for the Holy Spirit to help you in your weak areas. Next week we will look at the controversial topic of morality and see what Paul says about living a life of faith and victory over sin.

# NOTES ON MATTHEW 5:1–12

**Summary:** This is one of the best-known passages in Scripture. The difficulty is understanding what it means and how it can affect your life to live out these characteristics. Jesus held up a high standard in this sermon. This section gives an overview to the spirit or character of the member of the kingdom of God. To be a person living after the heart of God you need to understand what God's desire is. This list gives substance to the desired nature of a follower of Christ. It is a goal that is quite impossible without the grace of God.

**5:1 on the mountain.** To the original Jewish readers, this would have been an inescapable allusion to the time long ago when Moses climbed Mount Sinai and delivered the Law to Israel. **sat down.** Typically, when rabbis taught in the synagogue, they would sit rather than stand (like modern preachers). This also accents Jesus' authoritative position. **disciples.** This teaching is for everyone who would be a follower of Jesus.

**5:3–10** The "Beatitudes" are so named because in the Latin translation each of the eight statements begins with the word *beatus*.

**5:3 Blessed are.** The Greek word *makarios* refers to people who are to be congratulated. It does not necessarily mean they are happy or prospering. Instead, whether they feel it or not, they are fortunate because their condition reflects that they are in a right relationship to God. **poor in spirit.** This phrase does not refer to those who are poor in the material sense, but to those who acknowledge their need of God. Luke's version omits the words "in spirit." **the kingdom of heaven is theirs.** The Beatitudes assert that in Jesus this deliverance has come for all types of people who acknowledge their need and dependence upon God. Such is Jesus' message to any group who would assume that only certified members of that particular religious, racial or ethnic group are heirs to God's kingdom.

**5:4 those who mourn.** This does not refer to the bereaved, but to those who are in touch with the pain of the world caused by the pride, arrogance and evil of people who do not recognize their bankruptcy before God. In short, this is mourning over sin, both that which is intensely personal and that which is broadly social.

**5:5 the gentle.** This is similar in meaning to the phrase "the poor in spirit." It involves a lifestyle marked by meekness, humility and courteousness. **they will inherit the earth.** The irony of God's reign is that, despite the efforts of those who grasp for the world, it will one day be given over to those who have demonstrated a life of gentleness.

**5:6 hunger and thirst for righteousness.** As hungry or thirsty people devote their entire energy to finding food and water, so those in the kingdom are marked by a deep-seated, intense longing for knowing and living in God's way. **filled.** Because righteousness defines the very character of God, those who pursue it can be assured of the ultimate satisfaction of their desire when God's kingdom is manifested in all its fullness.

**5:7 the merciful.** Mercy is an act of deliberate kindness toward someone who has no claim upon the person rendering the kindness. **shown mercy.** Those who show mercy reveal that they recognize their own need for mercy. In this promise, Jesus assures them that they will indeed find mercy from God.

**5:8 pure in heart.** The call is for single-minded pursuit of God's way with every facet of our being. **see God.** In the Old Testament, this term described what it meant to experience God's favor.

**5:9 peacemakers**. This beatitude calls for an active involvement in bringing about reconciliation between those in conflict, whether at the societal or personal level (Ps. 34:14). True peacemaking involves seeking heart-to-heart reconciliation between people. It requires the rooting out of the causes of alienation and the disciplined practice of attitudes and actions that truly work for harmony to take their place. The cross of Jesus perhaps most solemnly illustrates the price of peacemaking. **sons of God.** To be called a son or a child of someone meant that a person's character was seen as a reflection of the master or teacher whom he followed. It is in this sense that those who work for peace will be acknowledged to be the children of God, since God himself is the author of peace and reconciliation.

**5:10 persecuted for righteousness.** This is the persecution that comes to those who pursue God's way in contrast to the way of the world. Many first-century Christians knew what it was like to be persecuted. **kingdom of heaven.** Just as this is the reward promised in the first beatitude, so it is also promised in the final beatitude. The kingdom of heaven sums up all the fullness of God's blessings to his people.

**5:12 Be glad.** Literally, "to leap exceedingly." This response is out of recognition that such mistreatment at the hands of the world is an indication that one is faithful to God. **reward is great in heaven.** "Heaven" is the way Matthew refers to God (3:2). The point is not that their reward will only be after death, but rather that it will be experienced in the presence of God.

# Session 2
# MORALITY

**Scripture** Romans 8:5-17

## LAST WEEK

In last week's session, we considered how the way we view the world (our paradigm) influences our character, attitude and values. We listened as Jesus taught us a whole new paradigm in his Sermon on the Mount. Today we will tackle the difficult issue of morality.

When we deal with issues of morality, we know there will be great discussions or heated arguments. There is a tension between the way things are (realities), and the way things should be (values). As people of faith, our responsibility is to emphasize the way things should be—the values that faith teaches us. This means we see moral issues through the glasses of our values, rather than the spectacles of society.

### Ice-Breaker : 15 min.
## CONNECT WITH YOUR GROUP

**Leader**
Begin this session with a word of prayer. For this particular Ice-Breaker activity have your group members divide into subgroups of three or four and take turns sharing their responses.

Where do you stand on the following issues? Place an "X" on each line to indicate where your opinion is best stated. Take turns explaining your responses on each topic.

ON LAW AND ORDER:
Lock the "losers" up. _____Educate and rehabilitate them.

ON DRUGS:
Just say no. _____ Make them legal.

ON ABORTION:
People should have a choice. _____Fetuses have rights, too.

ON CONDOMS:
Kids must protect_____They encourage promiscuity.
themselves.

ON SMOKING:
It's my right. _____Your right to smoke
stops at my nose.

## Bible Study : 30 min.
## READ SCRIPTURE + DISCUSS

**Leader**
Have a member of the group, selected ahead of time, read aloud the Scripture passage. Then divide into subgroups of three to six and discuss the Questions for Interaction.

Paul gives a thorough explanation of what the life of faith is all about in his letter to the Romans. He states that although believers are saved by grace (and do not have to live up to the Law), we still need to seek the Spirit's guidance. If we set our minds on the things of God first—no matter the pressing circumstances of life around us—we will have the moral center to deal with difficulties. Read Romans 8:5–17 and note how those who are led by the Spirit are children of God.

**Life Through the Spirit**

*⁵For those whose lives are according to the flesh think about the things of the flesh, but those whose lives are according to the Spirit, about the things of the Spirit. ⁶For the mind-set of the flesh is death, but the mind-set of the Spirit is life and peace. ⁷For the mind-set of the flesh is hostile to God because it does not submit itself to God's law, for it is unable to do so. ⁸Those whose lives are in the flesh are unable to please God. ⁹You, however, are not in the flesh, but in the Spirit, since the Spirit of God lives in you. But if anyone does not have the Spirit of Christ, he does not belong to Him. ¹⁰Now if Christ is in you, the body is dead because of sin, but the Spirit is life because of righteousness. ¹¹And if the Spirit of Him who raised Jesus from the dead lives in you, then He who raised Christ from the dead will also bring your mortal bodies to life through His Spirit who lives in you.*

*¹²So then, brothers, we are not obligated to the flesh to live according to the flesh, ¹³for if you live according to the flesh, you are going to die. But if by the*

*Spirit you put to death the deeds of the body, you will live. ¹⁴All those led by God's Spirit are God's sons. ¹⁵For you did not receive a spirit of slavery to fall back into fear, but you received the Spirit of adoption, by whom we cry out, "**Abba, Father!**" ¹⁶The Spirit Himself testifies together with our spirit that we are God's children, ¹⁷and if children, also heirs—heirs of God and co-heirs with Christ—seeing that we suffer with Him so that we may also be glorified with Him.*

**Romans 8:5–17**

 QUESTIONS FOR INTERACTION

**Leader**
Refer to the Study Notes at the conclusion of this session as needed. If 30 minutes is not enough time to answer all of the questions in this section, conclude the Bible Study by answering question 7.

1. Why do you think Paul wrote this passage?

2. In this passage, what does Paul say about the two options people have in living their lives? Where is the battle for the control of a person's life going to be fought—and won or lost?

3. What does Paul mean by being "in the flesh" (v. 9)? How are we to deal with "the flesh"?

4. Which of these ways of "the flesh" challenges you the most?
   ○ Controlling my anger.
   ○ Controlling my lust.
   ○ Controlling my mouth—not swearing.
   ○ Controlling my mouth—always telling the truth.
   ○ Reconciling a broken relationship.
   ○ Keeping my promises.
   ○ Other_____.

5. When unhealthy thoughts enter your mind, what have you found most useful in dealing with them?

6. What is God saying to you about morality in this passage?
   - ○ I need to get my mind set on "things of the Spirit" rather than "things of the flesh" (v. 5).
   - ○ I need to make sure I have the "Spirit of Christ" (v. 9).
   - ○ I need to admit that I have lived "according to the flesh" (v. 12).
   - ○ I need to let the Holy Spirit control my life (v. 13).
   - ○ I need to deal with my fears (v. 15).
   - ○ I need to accept my secure status as God's child (v. 16).
   - ○ Other_____.

7. In verse 15, Paul says we can relate to God as "Abba"—which could be translated "Daddy." How intimate is your relationship with God? How does (or could) your closeness with God help you live a moral life?

### GOING DEEPER:
If your group has time and/or wants a challenge, go on to these questions.

8. What does it mean to be "led by God's Spirit" (v. 14)? How do we know if the Spirit truly lives within us?

9. How have you suffered with Christ (v. 17)? In what way are you looking forward to being glorified with him?

## Caring Time : 15 min.
### APPLY THE LESSON AND PRAY FOR ONE ANOTHER

**Leader**
Bring the group members back together for the Caring Time. Begin by sharing responses to all three questions. Then share prayer requests and close in a group prayer. Those who do not feel comfortable praying out loud should not feel pressured to do so. As the leader, conclude the prayer time and be sure to pray for the empty chair.

Come together for a time of prayer now, knowing that God will grant you victory over "the flesh" through the Holy Spirit. Share your responses to the following questions and then support and encourage one another in prayer.

1. This past week did you feel more like a child of God or an orphan, and why?

2. In what areas of your life do you specifically need prayer support in order to "put to death the deeds of the body" (v. 13)?

3. Share something about being in the family of God that you are especially thankful for.

*P. S. Add new group members to the Group Directory at the front of this book.*

Today we looked at the difficult issue of morality and studied what Paul had to say to the Romans about this very topic. We were reminded to focus on God and seek the Holy Spirit's guidance, rather than let ourselves be influenced by the culture around us. We were also encouraged by the fact that we are children of God and will one day "be glorified with Him" (v. 17). In the coming week, pray every morning for the Holy Spirit's help in living your day to please God, rather than living to please "the flesh" (v. 8). Next week we will consider the topic of unconditional love and turn once again to the Sermon on the Mount to see what Jesus has to say about this challenging and rewarding way of living.

 NOTES ON ROMANS 8:5–17

**Summary**: This passage falls at the end of a long section on the need for and the way of salvation. Here Paul tells how a believer is to live. It starts with a mindset on living under the control of the Spirit and not under the control of the flesh and the world. Living by faith is a great theme throughout Paul's writings. There is an everyday reality to eternal life. We, as members of God's kingdom, are to be free from sin

**8:5 lives are according to.** There are two options: to be preoccupied with sinful desires or to be focused on the desires of the Holy Spirit. **think about.** Assumptions, values, outlook, desires, purpose—all that forms one's perspective on life. What a person thinks determines how one acts. One's conduct is guided by one's outlook.

**8:6 death ... life.** The two outlooks lead to two patterns of conduct that result in two spiritual states—death to

God (because sin separates one from him) or life in the Spirit.

**8:9** The distinguishing characteristic of the Christian is the indwelling of the Holy Spirit.

**8:10–11** The consequence of having the Spirit within a person is life: life now (v. 10) and life eventually for the mortal body (v. 11), when the Christian experiences bodily resurrection.

**8:12 obligated.** Christians have no further obligation to indulge their self-centeredness. Rather, they owe a debt to a life of holiness; i.e., they are obliged to live a life that is consistent with the life of the Spirit within them.

**8:13 put to death.** In Romans 7:4, Paul says that Christians are "dead to the law" via Christ's once-for-all act of dying on the cross in their place. In response to this fact, believers are daily (the verb tense indicates an action that is repeated over and over) to "put to death" all those practices they know to be wrong, all the attitudes that are not of God, and all the thoughts that would lead to sin. The presence of the Holy Spirit in one's life is not the end of the battle against sin but only the beginning, in the sense that now there is a hope of winning. **you will live.** This is the evidence that one has truly come to Christ and thus has the promise of eternal life.

**8:15 a spirit of slavery.** The Holy Spirit brings us, not into a new form of anxious bondage, but into union with Christ, enabling us to share his sonship. **you received.** The verb tense indicates that this is a one-time, past action—something that happened at conversion. **adoption.** The Roman practice of adoption was a most serious and complicated process, because a child was the absolute possession of his father. For a child to be adopted into a new family, he was first symbolically "sold" by his father to the adopting father. Then the legal case for adoption was taken to the magistrate. The end result was that the child: (1) lost all rights in the old family while gaining full rights in the new one, (2) became a co-heir in the new father's estate, (3) had all his old debts canceled forever, and (4) became in all senses the child of the new father. **cry.** In the Psalms this word is used of urgent prayer (Ps. 3:4). **Abba.** An Aramaic word used by children; best translated "Daddy," signifying a close, intimate relationship. **Abba, Father.** The very words Jesus prayed in the Garden of Gethsemane (Mark 14:36).

**8:16** In the Roman adoptive proceedings there were several witnesses to the ceremony who would, if a dispute arose later, verify that the particular child had actually been adopted. The Holy Spirit is the one who verifies a person's adoption into the family of God.

**8:17 heirs.** If someone is one of God's children, then that person is an heir, and will share in God's riches. In fact, Jesus is God's true heir, but since believers are "in Christ," they become sons and daughters of God by adoption, and thus are joint-heirs with Christ. **suffer.** The willingness to suffer for Christ is a mark of belonging. **glorified.** Christians have the hope of sharing in the reign of Christ over all creation.

# Session 3
# UNCONDITIONAL LOVE
Scripture **Matthew 5:38-48**

 ## LAST WEEK

We took on some tough moral issues in last week's session as we discussed the lifestyle that the culture around us promotes vs. the way God wants Christians to live. Paul gave us some insights, in his letter to the Romans, on how to focus on pleasing God rather than pleasing ourselves. We were reminded that the only way to accomplish this is to live by the Spirit. We also rejoiced in the knowledge that we are God's children and co-heirs with Christ, and are promised eternal joy and life. Today we will turn our attention to understanding what it means to love unconditionally.

Will Rogers once said, "I never met a man I didn't like." Many of us would reply, "Evidently, Will never met so-and-so." If we are honest with ourselves, there are people in our lives with whom we can't get along and whom we don't like. However, we are taught in Scripture to love all people, including our enemies.

The thought of loving someone who divorced us, cut us out of a business deal, told rumors about us or hurt us in some way seems beyond our abilities. And to "love" a murderer or a person who leads a nation with whom we are at war seems ludicrous. But Jesus did just that. He died to save everyone, even those who hated him. He even forgave the people who carried out his brutal crucifixion. So, we will turn to Jesus to teach us how to embrace unconditional love.

 ## Ice-Breaker : 15 min.
## CONNECT WITH YOUR GROUP

**Leader**
Welcome and introduce new group members. Be sure that everyone gets a chance to participate in the Ice-Breaker activity. Remember to stick closely to the three-part agenda and the time allowed for each segment.

When was the last time you recalled some of the times in your childhood that made you feel especially warm, contented and loved? Take turns answering the following questions and share some of your unique memories.

1. Where were you living between the ages of 7 and 12, and what was your favorite thing to do on a warm summer day?

2. Where was your favorite place to cuddle and keep warm on a rainy or snowy day? Where was your favorite place to hide during bad storms?

3. What was the center of warmth in your life when you were a child? (It could be a place in the house, a time of year, a person, etc.)

4. When did God become a "warm" person to you and a place of refuge during difficult times? How did that happen?

## Bible Study : 30 min.
## READ SCRIPTURE + DISCUSS

**Leader**
Have a member of the group, selected ahead of time, read aloud the Scripture passage. Then discuss the Questions for Interaction, breaking up into smaller subgroups of three to six.

As Jesus continues his Sermon on the Mount he addresses the issues of revenge and love. He totally rejects the thought of personal revenge and calls instead for loving one's enemies. Read Matthew 5:38–48 and note how Jesus defines love.

**Love for Enemies**

³⁸"You have heard that it was said, 'An eye for an eye' and 'a tooth for a tooth.' ³⁹But I tell you, don't resist an evildoer. On the contrary, if anyone slaps you on your right cheek, turn the other to him also. ⁴⁰As for the one who wants to sue you and take away your shirt, let him have your coat as well. ⁴¹And if anyone forces you to go one mile, go with him two. ⁴²Give to the one who asks you, and don't turn away from the one who wants to borrow from you.
⁴³"You have heard that it was said, 'You shall love your neighbor and hate your enemy.' ⁴⁴But I tell you, love your enemies, and pray for those who persecute you, ⁴⁵so that you may be sons of your Father in heaven. For He causes His sun to rise on the evil and the good, and sends rain on the righteous and the unrighteous. ⁴⁶For if you love those who love you, what reward will you have? Don't even the tax collectors do the same? ⁴⁷And if you greet only your brothers, what are you doing out of the ordinary? Don't even the Gentiles do the same? ⁴⁸Be perfect, therefore, as your heavenly Father is perfect.

**Matthew 5:38–48**

# ? | QUESTIONS FOR INTERACTION

**Leader**
Refer to the Study Notes at the conclusion of this session as needed. If 30 minutes is not enough time to answer all of the questions in this section, conclude the Bible Study by answering questions 6 and 7.

1. How did your parents resolve conflicts between you and your brother, sister or friend?
   - ○ They let us fight it out.
   - ○ They prayed about it.
   - ○ They yelled at us.
   - ○ They ignored it.
   - ○ They sat us down to talk about it.
   - ○ They took sides.
   - ○ They sent us out of the house.
   - ○ They really didn't care.
   - ○ Other_____.

2. When you get hurt in relationships now, what do you usually do?

3. What characteristic distinguishes a Christian from a non-Christian (v. 44)? What actions demonstrate this characteristic?

4. Which of these "enemies" would you have a hard time loving?
   - ○ Anyone from the IRS.
   - ○ My spouse's ex-spouse.
   - ○ Those I fought in war.
   - ○ Conservatives.
   - ○ Liberals.
   - ○ My ex-spouse.
   - ○ Persons of a different race.
   - ○ A rival at work.
   - ○ Other_____.

5. What is Jesus saying you should do to take control of the situation when your rights are being violated?

6. Think of someone who has hurt you in the past. What would your response be if that person walked into the room right now?
   - ○ I would get up and leave.
   - ○ I would seek revenge—maybe even physical harm.
   - ○ I would remind them how they hurt me.
   - ○ I would forgive and forget.
   - ○ I would silently pray for them.
   - ○ It would depend upon their attitude toward me.
   - ○ Other_____.

7. Since turning your life over to God, what effect has this had on your ability to love others—even those who hurt you?

## GOING DEEPER:
If your group has time and/or wants a challenge, go on to these questions.

8. What was Jesus' intent in saying, "don't resist an evildoer" (v. 39)?

9. What is your first reaction to verse 48? What challenge is Jesus presenting to you?

Caring Time : 15 min.

## APPLY THE LESSON AND PRAY FOR ONE ANOTHER

**Leader**
Begin the Caring Time by having group members take turns sharing responses to all three questions. Be sure to save at least the last five minutes for a time of group prayer. Remember to include a prayer for the empty chair when concluding the prayer time.

Comfort and encourage one another with this time of sharing and prayer. Begin by sharing your responses to the following questions. Be sure to offer any prayer requests and concerns before closing in prayer.

1. How did someone show you unconditional love this past week? How did someone "persecute" you?

2. How do you need God's help in showing unconditional love to a difficult person in your life?

3. What is something you feel God is challenging you to do as a result of our study today?

# NEXT WEEK

Today we focused on the difficult task of showing others, including our enemies, unconditional love. Jesus reminded us that we are not to seek revenge when someone has hurt us, but we are to love and even pray for this person. We certainly can't accomplish this on our own, but only by relying on God's love to work through us. In the coming week, make a list of those who have hurt you and pray for these people every day. If possible, try to show your forgiveness in some way. Next week we will discuss our spiritual formation and how we can continue to grow and mature in our faith.

# NOTES ON MATTHEW 5:38–48

**Summary**: At the heart of Jesus' teaching was the "golden rule." There is no doubt that Jesus taught a lifestyle of love and forgiveness. This emphasis of Jesus is to be our guiding principle in life.

**5:38 An eye for an eye.** This is said to be the oldest law in the world. It is found in the codes of Hammurabi, a king who lived in the eighteenth century B.C., as well as three times in the Old Testament (Ex. 21:23–24; Lev. 24:20; Deut. 19:21). The Law's original intent was not to require "an eye for an eye, and a tooth for a tooth," but to limit punishment to the extent of the crime. The scribes had transformed this Law that set limits on judicial actions into an individual's right to carry out revenge in one's private affairs. Thus, it appeared that one could seek to do harm to another person and still be a good follower of God's Law!

**5:39 don't resist an evildoer.** Jesus dismisses this misinterpretation of the scribes and calls instead for an attitude of nonretaliation. In this context, "to resist" means to oppose or fight back, or to seek revenge against someone who has harmed you. Love, as illustrated by Jesus' response to the abuse of the Roman guards (Matt. 27:27–31), absorbs and diffuses hate: It does not respond in kind (Rom. 12:19–21). Jesus' teaching here does not invalidate judicial practices that seek justice for crimes. The point is that injustice and evil are to be dealt with through the proper channels, and not made into personal vendettas. Nor does Jesus' teaching imply that one should never take measures to protect oneself or someone else who is being assaulted. What is prohibited is the seeking of revenge, the desire and action to harm another in order to get back at them for a wrong done against you. What is exposed is the pharisaic hypocrisy of using the Law to justify attitudes and actions the Law actually prohibited.

**5:40 coat.** The Law (Ex. 22:25–26; Deut. 24:10–13) prohibited a person from seizing a person's coat as the payment of a debt, since this woolen outer robe was used as a blanket at night. Jesus' call here is for his followers to give beyond what even the Law could require.

**5:41 forces you to go one mile.** Roman soldiers had the right to press civilians into service to carry their gear for a distance up to one mile (the Roman "mile" was 1,000 paces). The word used here is a technical term for such compulsory conscription.

**5:43 You shall love your neighbor.** Jesus quotes Leviticus 19:18, which was the basis for community relationships among the Israelites. **hate your enemy.** This command is found neither in the Old Testament nor in the Talmud. Some Old Testament passages even call for compassion toward enemies (Prov. 25:21). However, passages that spoke of God's ultimate judicial action upon those nations that threatened Israel (Deut. 7:1–2; 20:16–18; 23:5–6; Ps. 139:21) may have been misapplied in popular thought to justify personal animosity against those who are disliked, especially non-Jews.

**5:44 love.** The word used here is *agape*. This is love that shows itself not by what a person feels, but by what the person does. *Agape* love is benevolent action done on the behalf of another without the expectation of reward. **pray.** One way this sort of love is demonstrated is by praying for those who harass you.

**5:46 tax collectors.** Tax collectors grew rich by charging people more than what was required (only they knew what was demanded by Rome), keeping the excess for themselves. A tax collector was, therefore, considered to be a traitor to Israel, one who was made unclean by his contact with Gentiles.

**5:48 Be perfect.** The Greek word used for "perfect" is *teleios*, which means, "having attained the end or purpose." Therefore, people can be "perfect" if they realize that for which they were made, which is to reflect God's image, and hence to love. This commandment to be perfect defines the goal toward which God's children strive. It is not a goal they can ever reach (only God is and can be "perfect"); it is, however, a pattern that becomes the basis of how they seek to live.

# Session 4
# SPIRITUALITY

Scripture **Galatians 5:16–26**

 LAST WEEK

In last week's session, we looked at what Jesus had to say about unconditional love in his Sermon on the Mount. We found that we are to love our enemies and pray for them, just as Jesus did from the cross. We were also reminded that it is the distinct characteristic of a Christian to return good for evil and seek reconciliation instead of retaliation. However, this can only be accomplished if we let go of our own selfish feelings and allow God's love to reign in our hearts. Today we will consider the topic of spirituality and check out what direction our moral compass is pointing in this area.

In recent years, interest in spirituality has increased. Within Christianity, there has been a renewed interest in the ministry of the Holy Spirit and in the practice of spiritual disciplines. In our society, there also has been growth in the area of Eastern religions, Islam, the occult and the New Age movement.

However, this attraction to spirituality is nothing new. People have always been in search of a "higher power." Centuries ago, Augustine wrote, "There is a God-shaped vacuum in every person that only Christ can fill." Today, people are still trying to fill that vacuum—but often apart from Christ. True spirituality comes through participating in spiritual disciplines.

"Discipline" is not a word that we enjoy. Discipline involves setting goals, and following steps to achieve those goals. The word "self" is key. Self-discipline is part of kingdom living and part of the Christian life to which we are called. Paul understood this, and so we will turn to his letter to the Galatians where he discusses spiritual maturity and the importance of producing spiritual fruit in our lives.

## Ice-Breaker : 15 min.
## CONNECT WITH YOUR GROUP

**Leader**
Welcome and introduce new group members. Have each group member share his or her responses to the following questions.

The beauty of nature often helps us to connect with God and understand him in a special way. Take turns answering the following questions about feeling close to God through nature.

1. Describe a spot in nature that was special to you when you were a child.

2. To which of the following scenes from nature would you go if you wanted to feel close to God?
   ○ The ocean.
   ○ A forest.
   ○ A waterfall.
   ○ A sunny day.
   ○ A mountain.
   ○ A mountain stream.
   ○ A thunderstorm.
   ○ Other_____.

3. Psalm 89:11 states, "The heavens are yours, and yours also the earth; you founded the world and all that is in it" (NIV). Which of the following aspects of God's creation do you desire to draw from?
   ○ The ocean – In my low "tides" I want to believe in "high tides."
   ○ A mountain – I need to feel that some things are constant and unmovable.
   ○ A mountain stream – I need to feel peace in the midst of the rush.
   ○ A forest – I need to feel part of a community of life.
   ○ A waterfall – I need to feel God's power in my life.
   ○ A thunderstorm – I need to let loose the turmoil I feel inside.
   ○ A sunny day – I need to feel warm and invigorated.
   ○ Other_____.

## Bible Study : 30 min.
## READ SCRIPTURE + DISCUSS

### Leader
Select three group members ahead of time to read the Scripture passage. Assign each reader one paragraph: Reader One—verses 16–18; Reader Two—verses 19–21; Reader Three—verses 22–26. Then divide into subgroups of three to six for discussion of the Questions for Interaction.

As Christians, we owe much of our understanding of what it means to pursue spiritual disciplines to the apostle Paul. This passage is one of many in which Paul exhorts believers how to live. Read Galatians 5:16–26 and note the Holy Spirit's role in helping us to follow a spirituality that is pleasing to God.

**Life by the Spirit**

Reader One: $^{16}$I say then, walk by the Spirit and you will not carry out the desire of the flesh. $^{17}$For the flesh desires what is against the Spirit, and the Spirit desires what is against the flesh; these are opposed to each other, so that you don't do what you want. $^{18}$But if you are led by the Spirit, you are not under the law.

Reader Two: $^{19}$Now the works of the flesh are obvious: sexual immorality, moral impurity, promiscuity, $^{20}$idolatry, sorcery, hatreds, strife, jealousy, outbursts of anger, selfish ambitions, dissensions, factions, $^{21}$envy, drunkenness, carousing, and anything similar, about which I tell you in advance—as I told you before—that those who practice such things will not inherit the kingdom of God.

Reader Three: $^{22}$But the fruit of the Spirit is love, joy, peace, patience, kindness, goodness, faith, $^{23}$gentleness, self-control. Against such things there is no law. $^{24}$Now those who belong to Christ Jesus have crucified the flesh with its passions and desires. $^{25}$If we live by the Spirit, we must also follow the Spirit. $^{26}$We must not become conceited, provoking one another, envying one another.

**Galatians 5:16–26**

# QUESTIONS FOR INTERACTION

**Leader**
Refer to the Study Notes at the conclusion of this session as needed. If 30 minutes is not enough time to answer all of the questions in this section, conclude the Bible Study by answering question 7.

1. What kind of spiritual upbringing did you have as a child?

2. In your home, how openly is the Christian faith expressed (in practices like giving, praying, worshiping, fasting, etc.)?
   - We're very expressive, and want the whole world to know it.
   - We're pretty expressive, but don't make a lot of noise about it.
   - We're not outwardly expressive, but our faith is really sincere.
   - We're rather private when it comes to these things.
   - Who gave you the right to ask such a personal question?
   - Members of my family differ so much, that it's hard to explain.
   - Other_____.

3. If you could change your answer to the last question, how would you like to be able to answer the question?

4. In this letter, Paul has repeatedly warned the Galatians about being enslaved to legalism. What does he warn them about being enslaved to in this passage?

5. How can you and God's Spirit weed out the "works of the flesh" and grow the "fruit of the Spirit" (vv. 22–24)?

6. Comparing your spiritual life to a fruit tree, how are you feeling?
   - Young and green, but growing.
   - Healthy and productive.
   - Full of wild branches that need pruning.
   - Worn out and drained of life.
   - Other_____.

7. If you are going to get serious about your spiritual life, what do you need to do?
   - Set time aside daily for devotions.
   - Learn how to listen for God's voice.
   - Be committed to a group like this.
   - Rearrange my priorities.
   - Get involved in giving to others.
   - Other_____.

## GOING DEEPER:

If your group has time and/or wants a challenge, go on to these questions.

8. If the Spirit lives within us, why do we still lack spiritual discipline?

9. Is the list of "works of the flesh" in verses 19–21 representative or complete? Is anything less than sinless perfection damned, or just sin as a lifestyle (v. 21)? Can a person who lives this way be a true Christian?

## Caring Time : 15 min.
## APPLY THE LESSON AND PRAY FOR ONE ANOTHER

**Leader**
Be sure to save at least 15 minutes for this important time. After sharing responses to all three questions and asking for prayer requests, close in a time of group prayer.

Take some time now to bring each other comfort and hope by sharing prayer requests and special concerns. Before closing in prayer, take turns sharing your answers to the following questions.

1. On a scale of 1 (not at all) to 10 (completely), how much did you feel led by the Holy Spirit this past week? How does that compare to one year ago?

2. In what situations do you find it most difficult to "walk by the Spirit" (v. 16)?

3. What can you do in the coming week to be more disciplined about your spiritual development?

## NEXT WEEK

Today we were challenged by the words of Paul about living in the Spirit and what that means for developing our spirituality. We were reminded we should seek to always grow and mature in our faith, thereby producing fruits of the Spirit. In the coming week, develop a plan for incorporating more spiritual disciplines into your life like Bible study, prayer, giving and fasting. Next week we will concentrate on the importance of contentment and how worry can rob us of our time, energy and peace.

# NOTES ON GALATIANS 5:16–26

**Summary**: Paul gives us his spiritual common sense. The flesh and the Spirit are at odds with one another. We can't be a disciple of Jesus and be no different than those who don't follow Jesus. If we are people of the Spirit, then it should be evident in our lives.

**5:16 walk by the Spirit.** Let the way you live be directed by the Holy Spirit. It is the Holy Spirit, not the Law, who will bring about a moral lifestyle and spiritual discipline.

**5:20 idolatry.** The worship of any idol, be it a carved image of God (a statue) or an abstract substitute for God (a status symbol). An idol is identified as such because when faced with a choice, a person will follow its leading. Money becomes an idol when to gain it a person will do anything. **sorcery.** *Pharmakeia* is literally "the use of drugs," which was often associated with the practice of sorcery. **hatreds.** This is the underlying political, social and religious hostility that drives individuals and communities apart. **strife.** This is the type of contention that leads to factions. **selfish ambitions.** This word has come to refer to anyone who works only for his or her own good and not for the benefit of others. **factions.** This means the party spirit that leads people to regard those with whom they disagree as enemies.

**5:21 drunkenness.** In the first century, diluted wine was drunk regularly by all ages, but drunkenness was condemned. **anything similar.** The list is representative, not exhaustive—touching, in order, upon the sins of sensuality, idolatry, social dissension and intemperance. **not inherit.** The issue here is not sins into which one falls, but sin as a lifestyle. These are evidence of a life not controlled by the Spirit, and therefore the implication is that such a person has not been born from above and become a child of God.

**5:22 fruit of the Spirit.** These are traits that characterize the child of God. **love.** *Agape* (self-giving, active benevolence that is meant to characterize Christian love); in contrast, there is *eros* (sexual love), *philos* (warm feelings to friends and family), and *storge* (family affection). **joy.** The Greek word is *chara*, and comes from the same root as "grace" (*charis*). It is not based on earthly things or human achievement; it is a gift from God based on a right relationship with him. **peace.** The prime meaning of this word is not negative ("an absence of conflict"), but positive ("the presence of that which brings wholeness and well-being"). **patience.** This is the ability to be steadfast with people, refusing to give up on them. **kindness.** This is the compassionate use of strength for the good of another. **goodness.** This implies moral purity that reflects the character of God. **faith.** This is to be reliable and trustworthy.

**5:23 gentleness.** According to Aristotle, this is the virtue that lies between excessive proneness to anger and the inability to be angry; it implies control of oneself. **self-control.** This is

36

control of one's sensual passions, rather than control of one's anger (as in gentleness). **there is no law.** While it is possible to legislate certain forms of behavior, one cannot command love, joy, peace, etc. These are each gifts of God's grace. With this list of qualities, one moves into a whole new realm of reality, well beyond the sphere of the Law.

**5:24 have crucified the flesh.** It is via the Cross that a person dies to the power of the Law (Gal. 2:19). Paul indicates here that in the same way, a person also dies to the power of their sinful nature. The verb indicates that this is not something done to the Christian but by the Christian. The Christian actively and deliberately has repented of (turned away from) the old wayward patterns of life.

**5:25 live by the Spirit.** In the same way that the death of the ego (the "I" principle) is replaced by the mind of Christ (Gal. 2:20), here Paul indicates that the death of the sinful nature is replaced by the life of the Spirit.

# Session 5
# CONTENTMENT
### Scripture Matthew 6:19-34

 LAST WEEK

How do we keep growing and maturing in our faith? Last week we considered this question as we looked at the topic of developing our spirituality. Paul reminded us that we need to "live by the Spirit" if we want to produce spiritual fruit and conquer the "works of the flesh" (Gal. 5:16). The Spirit can also help us to follow through on spiritual disciplines such as Bible study, prayer, giving and fasting. All of these things will help us continue to grow in our faith and live out the Christian life to which we are called. Today we will turn our thoughts to the issue of contentment.

What can we do to increase contentment and decrease worry? We live in a culture that tells us our goals should include the accumulation of things, material wealth, power and prestige. Our world tells us to strive for more, but Jesus speaks of being content with what we have in this world. It's difficult to be satisfied with what we have—we always want something more.

Jesus reminds us that accumulating wealth or possessions, as a means of obtaining security in life, is incompatible with seeking God's kingdom. We know that we should be content with what we have in life. We know that we shouldn't worry about tomorrow or the future. But how can we be content when we have so many concerns in our life? We know that worry saps our time and energy. Besides, 90 percent of what we worry about never happens. Let's go once again to the Sermon on the Mount and see how Jesus puts worry in the right perspective

## Ice-Breaker : 15 min.
## CONNECT WITH YOUR GROUP

**Leader**
Be sure that new group members are introduced and welcomed. Have each member take turns sharing his or her responses to the Ice-Breaker activity.

If you could have three wishes, which three would you choose from the list below? Take turns sharing your wishes with one another.

- ○ **Win the Lottery:** Never have to work again.
- ○ **Secure Job:** Lifetime guarantee with benefits.
- ○ **Perfect Body:** Appearance that stands out in a crowd.
- ○ **Stress-free Life:** No pain, no struggle, no tension.
- ○ **Close Family:** No hassles, lots of love and support.
- ○ **Good Health:** Long life, full of vigor and vitality.
- ○ **One Deep, Abiding Friendship:** Someone who will always be there.
- ○ **Success:** Fame and recognition in your chosen field.
- ○ **Strong, Spiritual Faith:** A deep, satisfying relationship with God.
- ○ **Other** _____.

## Bible Study : 30 min.
## READ SCRIPTURE + DISCUSS

**Leader**
Select two members of the group ahead of time to read aloud the Scripture passage. Then discuss the Questions for Interaction, breaking up into smaller subgroups of three to six,

Jesus doesn't want our lives to be filled with stress and worry! The path to contentment means the believer must choose between two treasures (vv. 19–21), two visions (vv. 22–23), two masters (v. 24) and two attitudes (vv. 25–34). Read Matthew 6:19–34, which is from the Sermon on the Mount, and note what choices Jesus wants us to be making.

**Treasures in Heaven**

*19"Don't collect for yourselves treasures on earth, where moth and rust destroy and where thieves break in and steal. 20But collect for yourselves treasures in heaven, where neither moth nor rust destroys, and where thieves don't break in and steal. 21For where your treasure is, there your heart will be also.*

*22"The eye is the lamp of the body. If your eye is generous, your whole body will be full of light. 23But if your eye is stingy, your whole body will be full of darkness. So if the light within you is darkness—how deep is that darkness!*

²⁴"No one can be a slave of two masters, since either he will hate one and love the other, or be devoted to one and despise the other. You cannot be slaves of God and of money.

²⁵"This is why I tell you: Don't worry about your life, what you will eat or what you will drink; or about your body, what you will wear. Isn't life more than food and the body more than clothing? ²⁶Look at the birds of the sky: they don't sow or reap or gather into barns, yet your heavenly Father feeds them. Aren't you worth more than they? ²⁷Can any of you add a single cubit to his height by worrying? ²⁸And why do you worry about clothes? Learn how the wildflowers of the field grow: they don't labor or spin thread. ²⁹Yet I tell you that not even Solomon in all his splendor was adorned like one of these! ³⁰If that's how God clothes the grass of the field, which is here today and thrown into the furnace tomorrow, won't He do much more for you—you of little faith? ³¹So don't worry, saying, 'What will we eat?' or 'What will we drink?' or 'What will we wear?' ³²For the Gentiles eagerly seek all these things, and your heavenly Father knows that you need them. ³³But seek first the kingdom of God and His righteousness, and all these things will be provided for you. ³⁴Therefore don't worry about tomorrow, because tomorrow will worry about itself. Each day has enough trouble of its own.

**Matthew 6:19–34**

 | QUESTIONS FOR INTERACTION

**Leader**
Refer to the Study Notes at the end of this session as needed. If 30 minutes is not enough time to answer all of the questions in this section, conclude the Bible Study by answering question 7.

1. If you had heard this passage for the first time (and did not know that Jesus said it), what would have been your first reaction?
   ○ Sounds like a hippy from the '60s.
   ○ This person is out of touch with the modern world.
   ○ This guy doesn't have to support a family.
   ○ This is the kind of message our world needs.
   ○ I wish it were that easy.
   ○ Other_____.

2. How do you usually handle worry?
   ○ What, me worry?
   ○ I talk about it so much that others worry.
   ○ I get busy so I don't think about it.
   ○ I let go and let God take care of it.
   ○ I worry so much it worries me.
   ○ I give in to one of my vices to relieve the pressure.
   ○ I get professional help.
   ○ Other_____.

3. What specific things or situations does Jesus say we are not to worry about?

4. How content are you in each of the following areas of your life? Assign a percentage to indicate where you are—somewhere between 0% contentment (*Panic Button*) and 100% contentment (*No Problem*)—for each category:

   |  | 0% | contentment | 100% |
   |---|---|---|---|
   | My family. | 0 | _____ | 100 |
   | My self-worth. | 0 | _____ | 100 |
   | My relationship with God. | 0 | _____ | 100 |
   | My finances. | 0 | _____ | 100 |
   | My job/career. | 0 | _____ | 100 |
   | My relationship with friends. | 0 | _____ | 100 |
   | My health. | 0 | _____ | 100 |
   | The future. | 0 | _____ | 100 |

5. What are we to seek in place of material things (v. 33)? What pressures have tried to convince you to serve money?

6. If Jesus were to analyze your life, what do you think he would say your "treasure" is?

7. What do you need to do to "collect for yourself treasures in heaven" (v. 20) and find contentment?
   ○ Invest more time in loving people and less in loving things.
   ○ Give more money to the church and to people in need.
   ○ Talk to more people about Christ.
   ○ Be a better witness to my family.
   ○ Spend more time at church.
   ○ Make Jesus my first priority.
   ○ Other_____.

## GOING DEEPER:
If your group has time and/or wants a challenge, go on to these questions.

8. What are some indications that a person has become a "slave ... of money" (v. 24)? Is there a difference between loving money and enjoying the comfort that comes from money?

9. What does it mean to "seek first the kingdom of God and His righteousness" (v. 33) and how is this the key to contentment?

## Caring Time : 15 min.
## APPLY THE LESSON AND PRAY FOR ONE ANOTHER

**Leader**
Bring the group members back together for the Caring Time. Begin by sharing responses to all three questions. Then share prayer requests and close in a group prayer. Those who do not feel comfortable praying out loud should not feel pressured to do so. As the leader, conclude the prayer time and be sure to pray for the empty chair.

Prayer is a wonderful way to find contentment! Take some time now to share how God has been working in your life, and to support one another in prayer.

1. What did you worry about most during this past week? How did God help you to deal with that concern?

2. If you were to change one thing in your lifestyle that would help you to more fully "seek first the kingdom of God and His righteousness," what would it be?

3. In what area of your life did you have the lowest percentage of contentment in question 4? How can the group pray for your contentment to increase in that area?

## NEXT WEEK

Today Jesus reminded us that the path to contentment is to serve and trust God above all. He knows our needs, loves us unconditionally and will take care of us. In the coming week, whenever you start to worry or feel discontented, write your concerns down on a prayer list and pray about them often. Next week we will look at the area of relationships and see what James has to say about relating to others in a loving and healthy way.

# NOTES ON MATTHEW 6:19–34

**Summary**: Our Lord brings our focus onto the things of greatest importance. What will last beyond this world? What has importance to God? Jesus is not teaching that poverty is superior to wealth. Rather, he is teaching us to see this life through the eyes of one who is devoted to God and his purposes.

**6:19 treasures on earth.** Possessions as such are not forbidden, but accumulating wealth or possessions as a means of trying to obtain security in life is incompatible with seeking God's kingdom. **moth and rust.** The irony of building one's life around possessions was that even the most valuable treasures on earth were vulnerable to destruction by insignificant creatures like moths and mice. Even with today's protective devices, inflation, devaluation, stock market crashes, economic shocks, etc., can despoil a person's earthly treasure literally overnight.

**6:20 treasures in heaven.** These would include both relationships made eternal (1 Thess. 4:13-18), and a spiritual wholeness that comes from God's approval of us.

**6:21** The real issue is not about the size and amount of one's possessions, but one's devotion to them. While a wealthy person's obsession with material goods might be more obvious, people of modest means can also have their lives revolve around trying to maintain or augment the few possessions they have. This passage reveals that material possessions have the power to command a loyalty that rightly belongs to God.

**6:22 The eye is the lamp of the body.** As a light shows us the way through the darkness, so the eye is what allows us to see so that we might move and act freely. Both eye and heart are sometimes used in the Bible as a metaphor to describe the motivating principle that guides the way a person lives.

**6:24 slave.** While a person might work for two employers, he or she cannot belong to two owners. **hate.** This is not so much active dislike as it is a way of expressing the fact that loyalty to the one master makes loyalty to another master literally impossible. **money.** From *mamonas*, an Aramaic word that means possessions. God, who calls his people to "have no other gods before me" (Ex. 20:3), will not tolerate divided loyalty from his people. Dividing our loyalty between God and money turns money into a god.

**6:25 Don't worry**. When we are focused on that which cannot be taken away from us (treasures in heaven) we don't have to worry about what is essential. For the other things necessary in life, we need to trust in God's provision.

**6:26 Aren't you worth more.** This does not denigrate the importance of animals to God. It is because humanity has a special relationship and responsibility to the Creator that people (made in God's image and given dominion over the creation – Gen. 1) are "more valuable" than animals.

**6:29 Solomon.** This king of Israel was noted for his fabulous wealth (1 Kings 10:14–29). Even the simplest flower is adorned more delicately and attractively than the richest person.

**6:31 So don't worry.** As verse 33 indicates, the disciples of Jesus are to be busy, but their activity is to be centered on pursuing God's agenda; not simply meeting their own needs.

**6:33 But seek first the kingdom of God.** The supreme ambition of the Christian is that all he or she thinks, says and does be for the glory of God.

**6:34 tomorrow.** Worry generally has to do with the future, about what lies ahead. The disciple is to live one day at a time. **trouble.** Disciples are not promised a trouble-free life; they are, however, promised God's care.

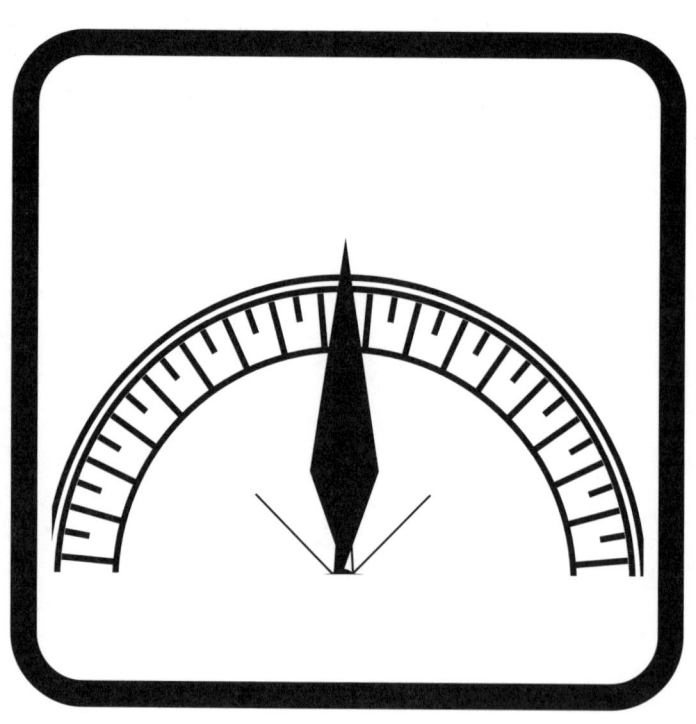

# Session 6
# RELATIONSHIPS

Scripture **James 4:1–12**

| **LAST WEEK**

Setting our moral compass in the direction of contentment instead of worry was our topic of discussion in last week's session. We once again turned to the words of Jesus from the Sermon on the Mount to help us understand how to be content with what we have in life. We were reminded that serving God rather than money is the only way to true happiness and freedom from worry. Today we will look at how we view relationships and interact with those around us.

A significant part of our lives is spent in relationship with others. As Christians, we are called to examine our perspective on how we relate to others. Again, the perspective of our culture conflicts with God's perspective.

One of the goals of incorporating God's core values into our lives is to help us mature. Maturity involves moving from a life of dependence (with the emphasis on "you"), to a life of independence (with the emphasis on "I"), and ultimately to a life of interdependence (with the emphasis on "we"). In today's study, James will remind us that we are to treat others as we want to be treated, and that relationships are a higher priority than our own desires.

## Ice-Breaker : 15 min.
## CONNECT WITH YOUR GROUP

**Leader**
Begin the session with a word of prayer, asking God for his blessing and presence. Then have each member take turns sharing his or her response to the Ice-Breaker activity.

How are you doing in your relationships with family and friends? From the following choices, select the answer(s) that best describes your recent behavior with first family and then friends. Take turns sharing your answers with the group. Then take turns sharing how you think your family and friends might describe you from the suggestions on the next page.

- **Mister Rogers:** I couldn't be nicer.
- **Mickey Mouse:** I listen so much I'm all ears!
- **David Letterman:** I make people laugh.
- **A Doormat:** People have been wiping their feet on me.
- **A Teddy Bear:** I seem to comfort people.
- **A Grizzly Bear:** Watch out! I might bite!
- **Aladdin's Genie:** All I do is grant other people's wishes.
- **Scrooge:** Keep your hands off my stuff!
- **Benedict Arnold:** I feel like a traitor.
- **Dracula:** People are afraid of me.
- **Your Pick:** _____.

## Bible Study : 30 min.
## READ SCRIPTURE + DISCUSS

**Leader**
Have a member of the group, selected ahead of time, read aloud the Scripture passage. Then discuss the Questions for Interaction, breaking up into smaller subgroups of three to six.

James, like Jesus, had some pretty strong things to say about relationships. The church he is writing to is having trouble because the members are not getting along. Their failure to live out God's love results in serious consequences for them as a church. Read James 4:1–12 and note how James exhorts them to live.

**Submit Yourselves to God**

**4** What is the source of the wars and the fights among you? Don't they come from the cravings that are at war within you? ²You desire and do not have. You murder and covet and cannot obtain. You fight and war. You do not have because you do not ask. ³You ask and don't receive because you ask wrongly, so that you may spend it on your desires for pleasure.

⁴Adulteresses! Do you not know that friendship with the world is hostility toward God? So whoever wants to be the world's friend becomes God's enemy. ⁵Or do you think it's without reason the Scripture says that the Spirit He has caused to live in us yearns jealously?

⁶But He gives greater grace. Therefore He says:

God resists the proud,
but gives grace to the humble.

⁷Therefore, submit to God. But resist the Devil, and he will flee from you. ⁸Draw near to God, and He will draw near to you. Cleanse your hands, sinners,

and purify your hearts, double-minded people! ⁹Be miserable and mourn and weep. Your laughter must change to mourning and your joy to sorrow. ¹⁰Humble yourselves before the Lord, and He will exalt you.

¹¹Don't criticize one another, brothers. He who criticizes a brother or judges his brother criticizes the law and judges the law. But if you judge the law, you are not a doer of the law but a judge. ¹²There is one lawgiver and judge who is able to save and to destroy. But who are you to judge your neighbor?

**James 4:1–12**

---

 ## QUESTIONS FOR INTERACTION

**Leader**
Refer to the Study Notes at the conclusion of this session as needed. If 30 minutes is not enough time to answer all of the questions in this section, conclude the Bible Study by answering question 7.

1. Who did you quarrel with the most when you were growing up and what about? Who do you quarrel with the most now and what about?

2. According to verses 1–3, what is at the root of "wars and the fights among you"? What are the reasons we don't have what we want?

3. What is your usual response when your desires are frustrated?
   ○ I fight and quarrel.
   ○ I throw a fit.
   ○ I commit it to God.
   ○ I covet what I don't have.
   ○ I give up.
   ○ I persevere until I get what I want.
   ○ I say, "I didn't want it anyway."
   ○ Other_____.

4. How do verses 7–10 improve our relationship with God?

5. Why is it wrong to criticize or judge others (vv. 11–12)? How does this affect our relationship with the person we are judging?

6. With which of the following persons are you likely to be most—and least—judgmental?
   - ○ My spouse.
   - ○ Other family members.
   - ○ People at work.
   - ○ Elected officials.
   - ○ Christians in general.
   - ○ Myself.
   - ○ My children.
   - ○ My friends.
   - ○ People at church.
   - ○ Celebrities.
   - ○ Non-Christians in general.
   - ○ Other_____.

7. Which of the following relational problems mentioned in this passage do you most need to work on?
   - ○ Fighting and quarreling (vv. 1–2).
   - ○ Coveting what someone else has (v. 2).
   - ○ Allowing myself to be influenced in a "worldly" way by others (v. 4).
   - ○ Criticizing, speaking against or judging others (v. 11).

### GOING DEEPER:
If your group has time and/or wants a challenge, go on to these questions.

8. When James uses the word "Adulteresses!" (v. 4) to describe these Christians, what is he referring to? How has their relationship changed with God?

9. What are some ways a person can "resist the Devil" (v. 7)? How can we help each other to do this?

Caring Time : 15 min.
### APPLY THE LESSON AND PRAY FOR ONE ANOTHER

**Leader**
Following the Caring Time, discuss with your group how they would like to celebrate the last session next week. Also, discuss the possibility of splitting into two groups and continuing with another study.

Praying with one another is a wonderful way to strengthen relationships. Begin by responding to the following questions, then share prayer requests and close in prayer.

1. How would you describe your relationship with Jesus this past week?
   - ○ Distant.
   - ○ Growing.
   - ○ Very close.
   - ○ Slipping.
   - ○ Other_____.

2. What step will you take in the coming week to improve your relationships with others and/or your relationship with Jesus?

3. In what area of your life do you need to "submit to God" and "resist the Devil" (v. 7)?

Today we looked at improving our relationships and dealing with some of the difficulties we often encounter in our interactions with others. James reminded us that becoming "the world's friend" and pursuing our own selfish ambitions is at the root of most of our relational problems. We were also given the promise that if we draw near to God, he will draw near to us (v. 8). In the coming week, take some extra time to draw closer to God in prayer and Bible study every day. In our next and final session, we will talk about the choices we make and how they reflect our commitment to Christ.

 **NOTES ON JAMES 4:1–12**

**Summary:** James is extremely practical. The reason for the problem was they weren't submitting to God. It is just the same way in our time. The readers wanted acceptance by the world and failed to show care for one another. The solution is simple: obey God and put your money where your mouth is. Do the work of the faith.

**4:1** This strife is not caused by persecution from the world. James is very clear that the strife is internal ("among you"). **wars and the fights.** These are long-term conflicts, not sudden explosions. cravings. Literally, "pleasures." James is not saying that personal pleasure is inherently wrong. However, there is a certain desire for gratification that springs from the wrong source and possesses a person in the pursuit of its fulfillment. **within you.** The struggle is within a believer—between the part of him or her that is controlled by the Holy Spirit and the part that is controlled by the flesh.

**4:2 You desire.** This is desire at work (James 1:14). **and do not have.** This is desire frustrated. **murder and covet.** This is how frustrated desire responds. It lashes out at others in anger and abuse. (This is "killing" in a metaphorical sense—Matt. 5:21–22.) It responds in jealousy to those who have what it wants. **fight and war.** This mad desire-driven quest causes a person to disregard other people, trampling over them if necessary to get what they want. **you do not ask.** One reason for this frustrated desire is a lack of prayer.

**4:3** The implication is not that God will not give us things that give us pleasure. God is the gracious God who gives not only bread and water but also steak and wine (Phil. 4:12). The point is that they are motivated by selfish desires and ask simply to gratify themselves. **spend.** This is the same word used in Luke 15:14 to describe the profligate behavior of the Prodigal Son.

**4:4 Adulteresses!** In Greek, this word is *feminine*, and probably refers to the people of Israel. By extension it refers to the church, the new Israel. In the Old Testament it was common to picture the relationship between God and his people as similar to the relationship between a husband and his wife (Isa. 54:5). To give spiritual allegiance to another ("the world") is therefore expressed in terms of adultery. **friendship with the world.** Rather than living in God's way, in the light of God's wisdom, his people are being molded by the values and desires of secular culture. They have, as it were, crossed over into the enemy's camp and decided to live there.

**4:6** But their case is not hopeless. God does give grace. Repentance is possible. They can turn from their misbehavior. **grace.** To receive grace, a person must ask for it. To be able to ask, one must see the need to do so. The proud person can't see such a need. Only the humble do.

**4:7 submit to God.** His first and primary command is that they must submit to God. It is not too surprising that James says this, since what these Christians have been doing is resisting God and his ways. **resist the Devil.** Submission to God begins with resistance to Satan. A clear sign of their new lifestyle will be this inner resistance to devilish desires. **he will flee from you.** Since Satan has no ultimate power over a Christian, when resisted he can do little but withdraw.

**4:8 Cleanse your hands.** Originally this was a ritual requirement whereby one became ceremoniously clean in preparation for the worship of God (Ex. 30:19–21). Now it is a symbol of the sort of inner purity God desires. **sinners.** Those whose lives have become more characteristic of the enemy than of God—lapsed or "worldly" Christians. **double-minded.** This is the parallel word to "sinners" and expresses nicely what life with two competing masters is like. God asks for singleness of purpose in His disciples.

**4:9 mourn and weep.** When people realize that they have been leading self-centered lives, in disobedience to God and harmful to others, they often feel overwhelming grief.

**4:10 Humble.** This last command urges humility before God, as did the first command ("Submit to God").

**4:12 one lawgiver and judge.** To judge others is to take to oneself a prerogative belonging to God. God is the Judge (Ps. 75:6–7) and the Lawgiver. **neighbor.** The Christian's duty to his or her neighbor is quite clear. It is to love, not judge.

# Session 7
# CHOICES

**Scripture** **Matthew 7:13–27**

 LAST WEEK

Even as Christians we sometimes struggle in our relationships with others. Last week we looked at this issue and got some very specific direction from James, as he outlined why we have conflicts with others. He reminded us that when we focus on the world, rather than God, our needs become more important than the needs of those around us. We then become covetous, hostile, critical and judgmental. On the other hand, if we submit to God and have a humble spirit our whole perspective on relationships will change and we will be able to love one another as Christ commanded. In our final session today, we will consider the importance of the choices we make and how they impact us today and for all of eternity.

Almost all of our choices, even the little ones, are influenced by the values we have decided to live by. What road are we going to take, and who are we going to follow? Once we choose to follow Christ and his way, then our values are part of our commitment to him, and they serve as an anchor in the midst of the hard times that come to each person's life. When everything around us seems about to fail, we can hold firm to Christ and the eternal values we have through him.

Our choice to follow Christ also helps us to look at the world differently because we now have an eternal perspective. Our priorities change because we know that our time on earth is only the beginning of a beautiful eternity with God. In our Scripture passage for today, Jesus instructs us to choose the narrow gate and path that leads to true life. Using another analogy, he tells us that in choosing him we now have a solid foundation on which to build, one that can weather any storm.

## Ice-Breaker : 15 min.
# CONNECT WITH YOUR GROUP

**Leader**
Begin this final session with a word of prayer and thanksgiving for this time together. Be sure to affirm each group member for the blessings and contributions that he or she made to the group.

Below is a list of qualities based on the positive values in this course. In silence, think about the members of your group and jot down their names next to the value that describes them best. Ask one person to sit in silence while the others explain which value they selected for that individual. Then go to the next person and do the same until everyone is affirmed.

_____ **Pure in Heart:** Your life is marked with integrity before God and other people.

_____ **Peacemaker:** You have a gift from God to help people overcome their differences.

_____ **Faithful:** You are faithful to uphold God's morality even under pressure.

_____ **Merciful:** You have the ability to feel what others feel; to be happy or to hurt with them.

_____ **Spiritually Hungry:** I admire the longing in your heart for a growing, genuine relationship with God.

_____ **Always Loving:** You have a Christlike capacity to love others unconditionally—no matter what.

_____ **Community Builder:** God uses you as a bond to bring people together in unity.

_____ **Humble:** I admire the quiet way you demonstrate what humility is all about.

_____ **Generous:** You give freely, not for attention or praise—but for the simple joy of giving.

_____ **Contented:** You know your worth is based on who you are rather than what you have.

_____ **Joyful:** Regardless of the circumstances, you have a smile on your face and a positive outlook about life.

_____ **Patient:** You never seem to be in a hurry or to get irritated by others.

# Bible Study : 30 min.
## READ SCRIPTURE + DISCUSS

**Leader**
Select a member of the group ahead of time to read aloud the Scripture passage. Then discuss the Questions for Interaction, breaking up into smaller groups of three to six.

The Sermon on the Mount is concluded by four contrasts in which Jesus urges people to choose between commitment to him and the way of the world. There are only two ways, two kinds of teachers, two kinds of followers and two kinds of foundations. Read Matthew 7:13–27 and note the results of choosing the way of the world.

**Wise and Foolish Choices**

$^{13}$Enter through the narrow gate; because the gate is wide and the road is broad that leads to destruction, and there are many who go through it. $^{14}$How narrow is the gate and difficult the road that leads to life; and few find it.

$^{15}$"Beware of false prophets who come to you in sheep's clothing, but inwardly are ravaging wolves. $^{16}$You'll recognize them by their fruit. Are grapes gathered from thornbushes or figs from thistles? $^{17}$In the same way, every good tree produces good fruit, but a bad tree produces bad fruit. $^{18}$A good tree can't produce bad fruit; neither can a bad tree produce good fruit. $^{19}$Every tree that doesn't produce good fruit is cut down and thrown into the fire. $^{20}$So you'll recognize them by their fruit.

$^{21}$"Not everyone who says to Me, 'Lord, Lord!' will enter the kingdom of heaven, but the one who does the will of My Father in heaven. $^{22}$On that day many will say to Me, 'Lord, Lord, didn't we prophesy in Your name, drive out demons in Your name, and do many miracles in Your name?' $^{23}$Then I will announce to them, 'I never knew you! Depart from Me, you lawbreakers!'

$^{24}$"Therefore, everyone who hears these words of Mine and acts on them will be like a sensible man who built his house on the rock. $^{25}$The rain fell, the rivers rose, and the winds blew and pounded that house. Yet it didn't collapse, because its foundation was on the rock. $^{26}$But everyone who hears these words of Mine and doesn't act on them will be like a foolish man who built his house on the sand. $^{27}$The rain fell, the rivers rose, the winds blew and pounded that house, and it collapsed. And its collapse was great!"

**Matthew 7:13–27**

# QUESTIONS FOR INTERACTION

**Leader**
Refer to the Study Notes at the conclusion of this session as needed. If 30 minutes is not enough time to answer all of the questions in this section, conclude the Bible Study by answering questions 6 and 7.

1. When you were growing up, who did your parents tell you to stay away from?

2. Where do the two roads in verses 13–14 lead? Which is the road less traveled and why?

3. Who are the "false prophets" that you need to be on your guard against?
   ○ The religious establishment.
   ○ Cults, New Age movement, other religions.
   ○ Those who have "fallen" in the Christian world.
   ○ Friends who don't have Christian values.
   ○ Other_____.

4. What is Jesus promising to the person who hears his words and "acts on them" (v. 24)?

5. In the past, what "sand" have you sometimes built your life upon?
   ○ My own abilities, resources or goodness.
   ○ Pleasing others.
   ○ Materialism—basing my happiness on things.
   ○ Pleasure—basing my happiness on good times.
   ○ Trendy philosophies.
   ○ Apathy—just going with the crowd.
   ○ Other_____.

6. How would you describe your spiritual foundation right now?
   ○ Shaky.                    ○ Solid.
   ○ Brand new.                ○ Slipping.
   ○ Rebuilding.               ○ Other_____.

7. What do you need to do most in order to build on "rock" in the future?
   ○ Learn more about growing in my faith.
   ○ Practice what I've already learned.
   ○ Change my priorities in life.
   ○ Stop worrying so much about what others think.
   ○ Plan for my future instead of acting on impulse.
   ○ Focus on my inner life rather than the externals of life.
   ○ Listen for God's voice and leading in my life.
   ○ Other_____.

## GOING DEEPER:
If your group has time and/or wants a challenge, go on to these questions.

8. Why is the gate so narrow and the road so difficult that leads to life (v. 14)? Why didn't God make it wider and easier?

9. How can someone do works in Jesus' name but not know him (vv. 22–23)?

Caring Time : 15 min.
## APPLY THE LESSON AND PRAY FOR ONE ANOTHER

**Leader**
Conclude this final Caring Time by praying for each group member and asking for God's blessing in any plans to start a new group and/or continue to study together.

Gather around each other now in this final time of sharing and prayer, being confident that God will give each of you the strength, wisdom and grace to build your morals, choices and values on the "rock" of Jesus Christ.

1. How has this group been a blessing in your life?

2. What are some specific areas in which you have grown in this course about core values and setting your moral compass?
   ○ Growing in my appreciation of God's Word as the standard for my values.
   ○ Increasing my commitment to Jesus Christ and his teachings.
   ○ Desiring to please God in regard to morality, values and choices.
   ○ Being more faithful to God's ideals for my relationship with others.
   ○ Longing to have a more intimate relationship with God.
   ○ Having a vision for how I can be more content in life.
   ○ Other_____.

3. What are some practical ways you can produce "good fruit" (v. 17) in the weeks to come?

# WHAT'S NEXT?

Today we considered the impact that the choices we make can have on our lives today and for all eternity. Jesus reminded us that we must choose between commitment to him and commitment to the way of the world. Building our lives on the "rock" of Jesus and his teachings leads to life and peace, while building on the "sand" of the world leads to destruction and separation from God. In the weeks ahead, take all of your decisions to God in prayer and ask for guidance in keeping on the narrow path of life and hope.

# NOTES ON MATTHEW 7:13–27

**Summary**: Jesus taught using parables and metaphors. In this passage, Jesus uses one metaphor after another to drive his point home: the gate, the wolf, the fruit tree, demons, the house built on rock all illustrate the need to follow God and to not take our cues from the world. The battle that we find ourselves in is important and our service is to the Lord.

**7:13 the gate is wide and the road is broad.** This is the way of the secular world that stands in contrast to the values taught in the Sermon on the Mount. **destruction.** This is where the "natural" way of the secular world leads. While ultimately such a lifestyle leads to the judgment of God against sin (Rom. 1:18), it also leads to destruction here and now, in the sense of estranged relationships and inner chaos.

**7:14 narrow is the gate and difficult the road.** The narrower road is the way of life advocated in the Sermon. This way leads to an inner wholeness marked by the presence of God and fulfilling human relationships. Following this road calls for discipline, training and faith. It also calls for people to go against the sinful tendencies of the broad road that seem so natural. Therefore, fewer people choose the more difficult narrow road. **life.** The narrow way is the path to eternal life with God, since it reflects the character of what that life entails. Jesus will refer to this destiny in verse 21 as entering "the kingdom of heaven."

**7:15 Beware.** Once again the disciple is called upon to make a judgment about other people. In this case, it is necessary to discern who speaks truthfully and who speaks falsely about religious truth. **sheep's clothing.** Prophets (like Elijah and John the Baptist) often wore animal skins (2 Kings 1:8; Matt. 3:4). People might dress in this fashion and (by doing so) claim to be prophets. Or, metaphorically, they might act as innocent as sheep while their true nature is that of vicious wolves who want to feed off others.

**7:20 by their fruit.** One important way to discern if a person is a genuine spokesperson for God is by considering what he or she does. Does the person reflect the values of the Sermon on the Mount in what they do?

**7:22 On that day.** This is the Day of Judgment. Throughout the Bible, there is a clear expectation of a final accounting of humanity by God. **'Lord, Lord, didn't we ...?'** Two important aspects of discipleship are accentuated in this verse: (1) Neither verbal allegiance to Jesus, nor powerful actions, nor success in ministry, nor the use of a certain type of "God-talk" can by itself be taken as evidence of a person being a true spokesperson for God. What really counts is whether that person is walking in the ways of God. (2) No one will enter the kingdom who attempts to do so on the basis of his or her deeds. These people tried to persuade the Lord to allow them access to his kingdom. The proper way to call upon Jesus as Lord is to acknowledge his sovereignty over all of one's life, look to him for mercy and humbly live in accordance with his teachings.

**7:24–27** In the autumn, rains produced flash floods that swept down ravines. While the two houses in the flood's path look alike, only the one built on a solid foundation will stand. In the same way, only those who build their lives on the foundation of loyalty to Jesus will stand through God's judgment.

# PERSONAL NOTES

# PERSONAL NOTES

# PERSONAL NOTES